Chapter 1 – A scary

The old chief was dead. The ~~villagers~~ needed a new leader.

"We need someone big and strong," said one villager.

"We need someone clever," said another.

An old woman spoke up. "What we need is someone who can speak up for us and ..."

Before she could finish a big, noisy boy shouted, "I'll do it! I'm a great talker. I'm brave. I've got lots of friends. I've got a big heart, big ideas and ..."

"... and a big mouth," muttered the old woman.

"I'll show you how great I am," boasted the boy. "Give me a task and I'll do it. I'm not scared of anything!"

Now at that time there was a problem in the village. This was the problem:

It was a silent slithery sly and scaly scary sneaky deadly snake!

This was one bad snake! One bite from its fangs and you were history. The snake was a deadly boomslang and it lived near the path to the river. Three villagers had been bitten by this snake. Three villagers were now dead.

The other villagers were too scared to go along the shady, tree-lined path to the river.

They knew what they wanted the big, noisy boy to do.

"Your task is to hunt and catch that deadly snake."

"Easy!" said the boy. "I'm not scared and I have lots of friends to help me."

So he and his friends went stomping and stamping, shouting and singing towards the path.

All day those boys stomped and shouted ... but they didn't even SEE the snake!

The next day, a second boy said, "I'd like to be our leader. Let me have a go. I can make a clever trap to catch that snake!"

"Let him have a go!" said the villagers.

"Yes," said the old woman. "But first I want to tell you something about ..."

The second boy wasn't listening. He was too busy planning his trap.

This is the trap he planned.

Snake Trap

Pull string to close trap door.
Also use as carrying handle.

block this end

snake

funnel entrance

stick to prop trap door open.

Log cut in half, hollowed and tied together with string.

It was a clever trap. It was made of good wood and strong string and … it didn't work at all!

At the end of the day this boy came back and all he had caught was one very smelly rat.

Then a third boy spoke up. "I'd like to try and catch that snake," he said.

"You don't look like a good leader!" said the villagers. "You're very short – and you're very quiet."

But in the end, they agreed that he could try.

"Listen!" said the old woman. The short boy listened. All that night when he could have been singing and dancing and boasting like the others, he sat and listened to the old woman.

This is what the woman said:

"I have lived a long time. I have seen many, many snakes. There is the bird snake and the black snake and the blind snake. There is the rock snake and the water snake. Then there is the tree snake. That is the snake we call a boomslang."

"A boomslang," said the old woman, "is big and sly – and deadly. One bite of its fangs and you're history."

"The best weapon you can have against a snake like that is *knowledge*. You must know all about it."

The boy continued to listen.

"The first thing to know," the woman said, "is that you will have to be very still and quiet. The boomslang can feel the shaking of the ground as you walk. Then it hides. That is why that noisy boy could not find it.

"The second thing to know is that this snake lives in trees. That is why the trap on the ground did not work. The boomslang likes to stay in the trees and eat the eggs of birds."

She talked all night.

Oh, that woman could really talk!

The boy listened.

Chapter 2 — To catch a boomslang

The next day the boy set off. He took a cloth bag stuffed with something. What do you think was in the bag? Aha! Wait and see.

The boy went up to the trees near the path. He sat down. Quiet and still, he listened. This is what he heard: the gentle *rushing* of a breeze in the grass, the twittering of a small bird, the **scurrying** of insects. Then he heard something else.

It was a quiet hissing sound.

The boy looked up. He saw a thin, brown-green branch twitch. But it wasn't a branch it was the snake!

It was sliding down the tree now, moving towards the boy. It was swelling up its neck, ready to bite.

The boy slipped his hand into his bag.
What did he have?
Was it an axe?
A knife?
A big stick?
No.
It was ...

an egg!

He rolled the egg towards the snake. With one gulp the snake ate it. Fatter now and slower, the snake slithered towards the boy.
The boy rolled another egg towards the snake. Gulp – the second egg was gone.

Slowly, quietly, the boy got up. He walked
carefully and he walked backwards. All the
time he kept his eye on the snake and all
the time he rolled eggs towards it. The
snake got fatter and fatter and slower and
slower but still it kept coming – all the way
back to the village.

"That short boy has no snake," the villagers laughed.

Then they saw the snake slithering through the grass behind the boy.

The boy rolled his last egg towards the boomslang and it stopped to eat. Then he threw the empty bag over it. The boomslang lay full and fed, still and sleepy under the shade of the bag.

"There is your snake," said the boy. "It is a deadly boomslang and I have hunted and caught it and brought it back to you."

The storyteller clapped his hands. "And that is how the boy who listened became our great leader!"

So that's my story, girls and boys.
Now up you get and make some noise.
I tell you stories new and old
Of clever kids and heroes bold.
Tales a-plenty I have to say ...
... but they are for another day.

Did you know ...?

Before writing was invented, people told stories to entertain and to pass on lessons about life. Stories were told from memory and were passed from generation to generation. That is why we often have different versions of the same story!

Boomslang facts

- Boomslang means 'tree snake'.
- The biggest boomslang ever found was 1.8 metres long! That's as long as your settee!
- Boomslang skin is one of the ingredients used to make Polyjuice Potion in *Harry Potter and the Chamber of Secrets*.

Snake jokes

Q: What is a snake's favourite subject at school?
A: Hissssstory!
Q: What kind of snake is good at maths?
A: An adder!
Q: How can you tell if a snake is a baby snake?
A: It has a rattle!